21st
Century
Skills Library

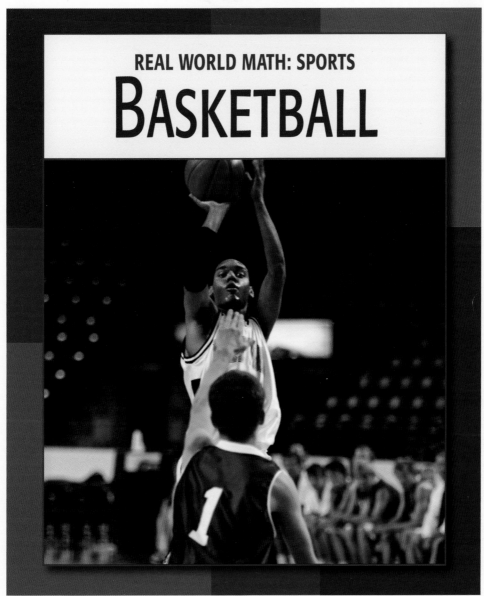

REAL WORLD MATH: SPORTS

BASKETBALL

Cecilia Minden and Katie Marsico

Cherry Lake Publishing
Ann Arbor, Michigan

Published in the United States of America by Cherry Lake Publishing
Ann Arbor, Michigan
www.cherrylakepublishing.com

Math Adviser: Tonya Walker, MA, Boston University

Content Adviser: Thomas Sawyer, EdD, Professor of Recreation and Sports Management,
Indiana State University

Photo Credits: Cover and page 1, ©iStockphoto.com/strickke; page 4, ©Nicholas Moore, used
under license from Shutterstock, Inc.; page 6, ©iStockphoto.com/cscredon; page 8, ©Peter
Casolino/Alamy; page 10, ©Pétur Ásgeirsson; page 12, ©GPI Stock/Alamy; page 15, ©Bob
Donnan/Robbins Photography; page 16, ©Brian Spurlock/Robbins Photography; page 19, ©AP
Photo/Douglas C. Pizac; page 20, ©AP Photo/John Swart; page 23, ©AP Photo/Tina Fineberg;
page 25, ©Mirenska Olga, used under license from Shutterstock, Inc.; page 26, ©iStockphoto.
com/MisterClips; page 28, ©iStockphoto.com/MaszaS

Library of Congress Cataloging-in-Publication Data
Minden, Cecilia.
Basketball / by Cecilia Minden and Katie Marsico.
   p. cm.—(Real world math)
Includes index.
ISBN-13: 978-1-60279-245-6
ISBN-10: 1-60279-245-3
1. Basketball—Juvenile literature. 2. Mathematics—Juvenile literature.
I. Marsico, Katie, 1980– II. Title. III. Series.
GV885.1.M56 2009
796.323—dc22   2008002042

Cherry Lake Publishing would like to acknowledge the work of
The Partnership for 21st Century Skills.
Please visit www.21stcenturyskills.org *for more information.*

TABLE OF CONTENTS

CHAPTER ONE

Hoop It Up!

Swish! Nothing beats hitting the final shot.

You feel the boards vibrating beneath your feet. Your **opponent** is in front of you trying to block your shot. You pass the ball to your teammate. The ball is passed back to you. You move toward the basket. You jump. Nothing but net! The crowd goes wild. The buzzer sounds, and the game ends. You made the winning basket!

Basketball is an exciting and popular sport. It is a fast moving and high

scoring game. Teams often score more than 100 points during a game.

That is a lot of math!

Today's sports have developed over time. They began as one game

and ended up as something very different. Dr. James Naismith created

basketball in 1891 in Springfield, Massachusetts. He wanted to create a

ball game that people could play indoors during the winter months. An

indoor game, however, meant the playing field would have to be smaller.

Naismith could not spread out, so he went up. He nailed peach baskets

REAL WORLD MATH CHALLENGE

Former NBA player Manute Bol is 7 feet 7 inches (2.31 m) tall. He weighs 225 pounds (102 kilograms). One of the league's shortest players, Tyrone Curtis "Muggsy" Bogues, measures 5 feet 3 inches (1.6 m) and weighs 136 pounds (62 kg). **How much taller is Bol than Bogues? How much lighter is Bogues than Bol?**

(Turn to page 29 for the answers)

The height of many basketball hoops can be adjusted. The standard height is 10 feet (3 m).

10 feet (3 meters) up on the wall of the gym. He then created 13 rules to get teams to work together.

Today, the National Basketball Association (NBA) is the primary organization for **professional** men's basketball in the

United States. It also has offices around the world.

The Women's National Basketball Association (WNBA) governs professional women's teams. The National Collegiate Athletic Association (NCAA) is the primary organization for college basketball. Students 18 years of age and under usually play in school or city leagues.

The size of the court, the height of the basket, and the score are all ways math matters to the game. And don't forget about the size of the players! Grab your calculator and let's play ball!

Learning & Innovation Skills

The peach basket was a good idea, but after every score, someone had to climb up a ladder to retrieve the ball. Using critical thinking and problem-solving skills, players came up with an idea. They cut out the bottom of the basket. This let the ball drop through to the floor. It worked for a while, but the baskets didn't last for many games! A net was added to guide the ball. The rest, as they say, is history.

CHAPTER TWO

A Few Basketball Basics

Basketball is a very physical game.

The object of basketball sounds pretty simple. Get the ball in the basket. But that basket is 10 feet (3 m) off the ground. And some very tall people are blocking your shot. So how does this game work?

Two teams compete against each other to see which team can score more points by the end of the game. They play on a court with a hoop at each end. The metal hoops are 18 inches (46 centimeters) in diameter. A net hangs from the hoop,

creating a basket. The object is to get the ball into the basket. The team

with the ball is on **offense**. The team without the ball is on **defense**. Players

on defense try to keep those on offense from making a shot.

The length of a basketball game varies according to the age and

experience of the players. Games for most middle-school players last 24

minutes. International, NCAA, and WNBA games are 40 minutes. NBA

games are 48 minutes. There is a 15-minute halftime break for NCAA,

WNBA, and NBA games. NBA teams have 12 members. Other teams have

10 members. During the game, five members from each team are on the

court. Coaches change players throughout the game.

Each time a player gets the ball in the basket, he scores 2 points. If the

player shoots and makes a basket from outside the 3-point line, then he

The 3-point shot is one of the toughest skill shots in basketball.

scores 3 points. In the NBA, this line is between 22 feet (6.7 m) and 23 feet 9 inches (7.2 m) from the basket. In college, women's, and international play, the 3-point line is about 20 feet (6 m) from the basket.

Fouls are given to players by referees for illegal body contact or behaving badly. Depending on the foul, the other team might get the ball or a chance at a free throw, a shot taken from the free throw line without interference. A team gains 1 point if the ball goes through the basket on a free throw. A player who commits five fouls during an NCAA game is **disqualified**. In the NBA, a player who commits six fouls is disqualified. Coaches can also be charged with fouls. After two fouls, a coach is ordered off the court.

REAL WORLD MATH CHALLENGE

NBA/NCAA **regulation** basketball courts are 94 feet (29 m) long by 50 feet (15 m) wide. High-school courts are 84 feet (26 m) long by 50 feet (15 m) wide. Middle-school courts measure 74 feet (23 m) long by 42 feet (13 m) wide. **How much longer is the high-school court than the middle-school court? How much wider? How many square feet is an NBA/NCAA court?**

(Turn to page 29 for the answers)

In 1992, top players from many NBA teams who normally competed against one another came together to play for the Olympics. Superstars on each team were all equal on the Olympic team. It was nicknamed America's Dream Team. The players were flexible and were willing to make compromises. They gave up individual needs to work as a team and bring home the Olympic gold.

Coaches and players need to be aware of fouls and keep track of how many the team has at any given time.

Players can play different positions depending on where they are needed in the game. The positions are point guard, shooting guard, small forward, power forward, and center. The point guard is a strong leader who runs the team on the court and needs

12

to be able to make quick decisions. The shooting guard must be able to make long outside shots and is often the top scorer on the team. A small forward is able to guard different positions well and usually defends against the opponent's best player. A power forward is good at blocking shots and clearing out players under the basket for rebounds. (A rebound occurs when a player attempts a shot and misses, and a player on his team recovers the ball.) The center is the tallest person on the team and is usually a high scorer who can block shots and catch rebounds.

All the positions require excellent basketball-handling skills, such as dribbling, passing, shooting, and catching rebounds. Dribbling means bouncing the ball without stopping. A player must be able to do this while traveling down the court. When you stop dribbling, you cannot put the ball back on the floor. You must shoot or pass the ball.

Players practice these skills in drills so they can move quickly on the court. You can, too. Dribble for one minute without looking at the ball. Count the number of times the ball hits the floor. Rest for 30 seconds. Repeat these three steps. Were you able to dribble faster the second time? Try it again. You are using your math skills to improve your basketball skills!

Professional basketball players continue to practice their skills even after they become major players. Let's read about some of the impressive professionals who make basketball such an exciting game.

CHAPTER THREE

DO THE MATH: IMPRESSIVE PROS

Few people would argue that the top basketball player of all time is Michael Jordan. At 6 feet 6 inches (1.98 m), Jordan wasn't the tallest player in the NBA, but few could match his skills on the court. His nickname was "Air" Jordan for his ability to almost float toward the basket to score.

Michael Jordan played for the University of North Carolina before turning pro and joining the Chicago Bulls in 1984.

In college, Jordan played for the University of North Carolina Tar Heels. His skills wowed the crowd during an NCAA Championship game

*Michael Jordan led the Bulls
to three NBA Championships
in 1991, 1992, and 1993.*

against Georgetown University in March 1982. As a freshman, Jordan made the winning basket in the last 18 seconds of the game with a 16-foot (4.9 m) jump shot. The Tar Heels won with a 63–62 victory. It is still called "The Shot."

Jordan's career in the NBA started in 1984 when he was drafted by the Chicago Bulls. He led the Bulls to six NBA Championship wins. He was named the NBA's Most Valuable Player (MVP) in 1988, 1991, 1992, 1996, and 1998. He also led the NBA in scoring for 10 seasons. In 1984 and 1992, he helped bring home the gold at the Olympics. In 1996, Jordan was named one of the top 50 basketball players of all time. He's at the top of the NBA all-time list for most points per game (PPG) with 30.1. Jordan retired from playing basketball in 2003.

REAL WORLD MATH CHALLENGE

Michael Jordan has earned millions of dollars on product **endorsements**. The biggest is for Nike Air Jordan athletic shoes. A pair of Air Jordan XX2 shoes sells for $174.99. Kadir is saving $17.25 a week to buy the shoes. **How long will it take him to purchase a pair of Air Jordan XX2 shoes?** Don't forget the 8 percent sales tax.

(Turn to page 29 for the answer)

One of the outstanding stars of the WNBA is Lisa Leslie. Standing 6 feet 5 inches (1.96 m), Leslie played college basketball for the University of Southern California (USC) and was named All-American her last three years there. When she graduated from USC in 1994, there wasn't a women's professional basketball league in the United States. She accepted a job playing for a team in Italy because she wanted to keep her skills sharp

to compete in the Olympics. In 1996, Leslie and her American teammates

brought home the Olympic gold. She helped bring home the gold again in

the 2000 and 2004 Olympics.

In 1997, soon after the WNBA was formed, Leslie signed on with the

Los Angeles Sparks. And by 2001, the Sparks ignited. They won the WNBA

Championship, and Leslie averaged 23.5 PPG in the finals. She earned All-

Star Game MVP, league MVP, and MVP of the WNBA Finals. She helped

her team repeat the win in 2002.

REAL WORLD MATH CHALLENGE

In 2007–2008, Los Angeles Lakers guard Kobe Bryant's contract was for $19,490,625. WNBA stars have a salary cap, or limit, of $93,000. **How much more money did Bryant make in 2008 than the top-paid WNBA player could earn? How many top-paid WNBA players' salaries could be paid with Bryant's salary?**

(Turn to page 29 for the answers)

*Lisa Leslie celebrates winning
Olympic gold in 2004.*

The International
Basketball Federation
was created in 1932
to promote the game
worldwide. Traveling
to other countries
has helped players
understand other
nations, cultures,
and languages. The
federation sponsors the
World Championship
Games every four years.

Leslie has her sights set on the 2008 Olympics.

She may bring home yet another gold medal!

Jordan and Leslie racked up impressive scores

throughout their careers. Basketball is a team sport,

however, and no one can win a game alone. Let's see

what other players work with big numbers!

CHAPTER FOUR

DO THE MATH: REMARKABLE BASKETBALL RECORDS

Magic Johnson played his entire career with the Los Angeles Lakers. He was elected to the Naismith Memorial Basketball Hall of Fame in 2002.

Earvin "Magic" Johnson was drafted by the Los Angeles Lakers in 1979.

He played for them for his entire 13-year career. Johnson helped the Lakers

win five NBA Championships in the 1980s. He was voted NBA MVP in

1987, 1989, and 1990. He played on the Dream Team and won Olympic gold in 1992. He was named one of the 50 Greatest Players in NBA History in 1996. He holds the all-time NBA record for assists per game. (Assists involve helping other players get the ball in the basket.)

Basketball is a fast-paced game. By the time you read this book, there will be new players who might beat the records of Jordan and Johnson. One top player is Kevin Garnett. Garnett plays power forward on the Boston Celtics. He is one of only five NBA players who have racked up more than 19,000 points, 10,000 rebounds, and 4,000 assists.

REAL WORLD MATH CHALLENGE

In 2005, Kevin Garnett donated $1.2 million to build 1 home a month for 2 years for victims of Hurricane Katrina. **How many homes will there be when all the homes are finished? What was the average contribution toward each home?**

(Turn to page 29 for the answers)

Dawn Staley, who stands 5 feet 6 inches (1.7 m), was a power force on the court long before she was a pro. While playing for the University of Virginia (1989–1992), she recorded 454 steals, an NCAA record. She joined the WNBA's Charlotte Sting in 1999. In 2004, she captured her third Olympic gold medal in Athens, Greece. Staley retired from playing basketball in 2006.

Another WNBA superstar, Sheryl Swoopes began her career at Texas Tech University. During the 1992–1993 season, she set an all-time scoring record for a single season with 955 points. Along with Leslie and Staley, Swoopes was on the Olympic teams for

1996, 2000, and 2004. She signed with the Houston Comets in 1997 and helped lead that team to four consecutive championship games from 1997 through 2000. She was voted the league's MVP for 2000, 2002, and 2005. Swoopes, who is 6 feet (1.8 m) tall, is the first player in WNBA history

Sheryl Swoopes takes a shot during a game in 2005.

to score a triple-double during playoffs. A triple-double is when a player earns 10 or more rebounds, points, and assists. Swoopes has sometimes been called "a female Michael Jordan." Like Jordan, she has a shoe—Air

Swoopes—named for her.

These are but a few of the many talented people who play basketball.

You can use math to understand just how remarkable their achievements

are. Remember, though, that each of these famous players began just like

you. They played in their neighborhoods, parks, and local gyms. Let's see

how you can use numbers to get on the boards.

REAL WORLD MATH CHALLENGE

Kim wants to buy cards of her 3 favorite players. A 1994 Dawn Staley card costs $19.95. A 2000 Lisa Leslie card costs $8.00. A 1999 Sheryl Swoopes card costs $23.31. Kim has $40.00. **Which cards can she buy? How much does she need to purchase all 3 cards**?

(Turn to page 29 for the answers)

CHAPTER FIVE

GET YOUR OWN GAME GOING!

Playing basketball with friends is a great way to improve your game.

Do you think you might someday play with the professionals? You can play right now with your friends and classmates. All you need is a hoop, a basketball, and players.

It is best to wear a loose-fitting cotton T-shirt and shorts when playing basketball. Each team should wear a specific color, so players can easily spot their teammates. Athletic socks and shoes will keep your feet safe. Be sure your shoes fit and are comfortable. Style is great, but it is more important to have good support for your ankles.

A good pair of shoes, a basketball, and comfortable clothes are basic basketball gear.

You might run into other players, so wear a mouth guard. If you wear glasses, make sure they are secure. You can purchase a special band that attaches to the earpieces on your glasses. It will keep your glasses from coming off during the game. Knee guards also help to prevent injury.

You have your gear. What now? Develop your skills. It is time to practice. You need to put in a lot of time to become a skilled player.

Let's say you join a local league that runs for six weeks. You have practices twice a week. Each practice lasts one hour. You have 10 games. Games last about an hour. That is a total of 22 hours of basketball over six weeks. But don't forget about practicing every day at home! Using your math skills, you can see that becoming a good player takes many hours of hard work.

Do you think you have what it takes to be the next Jordan or Swoopes? If so, maybe you'll face some of today's basketball superstars, such as Diana Taurasi of the Phoenix Mercury or LeBron James of the Cleveland Cavaliers.

21st Century Content

Staying healthy is the first step toward being a successful athlete. This includes eating right, exercising, and avoiding injuries. Get plenty of sleep. Snack on fresh fruit instead of candy bars. Always stretch and warm up before you play a game. Wear protective gear to cut down on injuries. Drink lots of water, especially if you are playing outside on a hot day. Never play if you are sick or in pain.

REAL WORLD MATH CHALLENGE

Coach Bristow is figuring out the averages for his local team. The team has played 4 games. Nick has scored 13, 6, 4, and 11 points per game. Anthony has scored 12, 11, 8, and 7. **Who has a higher PPG for the first 4 games?**

(Turn to page 29 for the answer)

All of these outstanding players have two things in common. They all use basketball skills and math skills to help them improve their playing and score big. Now it is your turn. Grab your basketball and hit the court.

The best players spend a lot of time practicing their skills!

Count those drills and practice those 3-point shots. Next time we read about an NBA or WNBA superstar, it could be you!

REAL WORLD MATH CHALLENGE ANSWERS

Chapter One
Page 5

Bol is 2 feet 4 inches (0.71 m) taller than Bogues.

7 feet − 5 feet = 2 feet

7 inches − 3 inches = 4 inches

Bogues is 89 pounds (40 kg) lighter than Bol.

225 pounds − 136 pounds = 89 pounds

Chapter Two
Page 11

The high-school court is 10 feet (3 m) longer than the middle-school court.

84 feet − 74 feet = 10 feet

It is 8 feet (2 m) wider.

50 feet − 42 feet = 8 feet

The NBA/NCAA court is 4,700 square feet.

Area = length x width

Area = 94 feet x 50 feet = 4,700 square feet

Chapter Three
Page 17

The sales tax comes to a total of $14.00.

$174.99 x 0.08 = $14.00

Kadir has to save $188.99.

$174.99 + $14.00 = $188.99

It will take him 11 weeks to have enough money for the Nike Air Jordans.

$188.99 ÷ $17.25 = 10.96 = 11 weeks

Page 18

Bryant earned $19,397,625 more than the top WNBA player.

$19,490,625 − $93,000 = $19,397,625

Bryant's salary could cover the salaries of 209 top-paid WNBA players.

$19,490,625 ÷ $93,000 = 209.6 = 209 players

Chapter Four
Page 21

There are 12 months in 1 year. In 1 year, 12 homes could be built. Garnett will therefore build 24 homes.

12 homes x 2 years = 24 homes

The average contribution to each home is $50,000.

$1,200,000 ÷ 24 homes = $50,000 per home

Page 24

Kim can purchase 2 cards. She can either purchase the Staley and Leslie cards for a total of $27.95 or the Leslie and Swoopes cards for $31.31.

For the Staley and Leslie cards: $19.95 + $8.00 = $27.95

For the Leslie and Swoopes cards: $8.00 + $23.31 = $31.31

She will need $11.26 more to purchase all 3 cards.

$19.95 + $8.00 + $23.31 = $51.26

$51.26 − $40.00 = $11.26

Chapter Five
Page 28

Anthony's PPG of 9.5 is higher than Nick's PPG of 8.5.

Anthony: 12 points + 11 points + 8 points + 7 points = 38 points

38 points ÷ 4 games = 9.5 points per game

Nick: 13 points + 6 points + 4 points + 11 points = 34 points

34 points ÷ 4 games = 8.5 points per game

GLOSSARY

defense (DEE-fenss) a team that is attempting to prevent its opponents from scoring

dimension (duh-MEN-shun) a measurement in more than one direction

disqualified (dis-KWA-leh-fyde) not eligible to play because of a rule violation

endorsements (en-DORS-mints) money earned from recommending a product

offense (AW-fenss) a team that is attempting to score

opponent (uh-POH-nuhnt) player on the other side or opposite team

professional (pruh-FESH-uh-nuhl) describing a sport that is played for money or as a career

regulation (reg-u-LAY-shun) rules issued by the organization governing a sport

FOR MORE INFORMATION

Books

Stewart, Wayne. *Little Giant Book of Basketball Facts.*
New York: Sterling Publishing, 2005.

Thomas, Keltie, and Greg Hall (illustrator). *How Basketball Works*. Toronto: Maple Tree Press, 2005.

Web Sites

Kids World Sports: Basketball
www.pbskids.org/kws/sports/basketball.html
Find out more about the game of basketball

NBA.com
www.nba.com
Get the latest information on your favorite NBA teams and players

Official Site of the NCAA Kids Club
www.ncaa.org/bbp/basketball_marketing/kids_club/
Links to basketball games and activities along with information on rules and tips on becoming a better player

INDEX

ABOUT THE AUTHORS

Cecilia Minden, PhD, is a former classroom teacher and university professor. She now enjoys being a literacy consultant and author of children's books. She lives with her family near Chapel Hill, North Carolina. Dr. Minden would like to dedicate this book to her son, David, one of basketball's biggest fans.

Katie Marsico worked as a managing editor in children's publishing before becoming a freelance writer. She lives near Chicago, Illinois, with her husband and two children. She is much better at dribbling and passing than scoring.